WELCOME TO THE WORLD OF
Sharks

Diane Swanson

Whitecap Books
Vancouver / Toronto

Edited by Elizabeth McLean
Cover design by Steve Penner
Interior design by Margaret Ng
Typeset by Maxine Lea and Jacqui Thomas
Photo credits: Neil G. McDaniel Photography iv, 4, 6, 16, 22, 24;
David Doubilet/First Light 2; Nick Caloyianis 8, 10, 14, 26;
David Fleetham/First Light 12; K.Aitken/First Light 18; Graeme Eisenhofer 20.

Printed and bound in Canada

National Library of Canada Cataloguing in Publication Data

Swanson, Diane, 1944–
     Welcome to the world of sharks

     Includes index.
     ISBN 1-55285-170-2

     1. Sharks—North America—Juvenile literature. I. Title.
QL638.9.S92 2001   j597.3'097   C2001-910174-0

For more information on
this series and other
Whitecap Books titles,
visit our web site at
www.whitecap.ca

The publisher acknowledges the support of the Canada Council for the Arts and the Cultural Services Branch of the Government of British Columbia for our publishing program. We acknowledge the financial support of the Government of Canada through the Book Publishing Industry Development Program for our publishing activities.

Contents

World of Difference

SHARKS RULE THE SEA. They're top-notch hunters with few enemies—but no wonder. Most sharks are master swimmers, able to charge powerfully through the water. And they possess a set of super senses for finding food and dodging danger.

Worldwide, there are 350 to 400 different kinds of sharks, and more than 100 kinds spend time off the coasts of Canada, the United States, and Mexico. Biggest of all are the whale sharks. They can be as long as two or three cars placed end to end! One of the smallest sharks is the cigar shark, a deep-water fish only

A large school of scalloped hammerheads gathers in warm waters.

1

A diver approaches a slow-swimming whale shark. As big as it is, it doesn't eat people.

about the length of a cigar. In most shark families, females are larger than males.

Sharks usually come in dull colors, such as gray-blue and gray-green. That makes them hard to spot—from above or below—which helps them hunt and stay clear of enemies.

Many sharks are shaped like rockets.

However, angel sharks have flat bodies—like the shark's close relatives, the skates and rays. Sawsharks have long, sawlike snouts with sharp teeth along the edges. And hammerhead sharks have heads shaped like hammers, with eyes and nostrils at both ends of the "hammers."

Look beneath a shark's head to find its wide, curved mouth—but it's not always there. The strange frill shark, for instance, has a mouth that's more like a snake's—right out in front.

SHARK SMARTS

Sharks are smart enough to learn as fast as rats can. Some have mastered tricks, such as slipping hoops over their heads, to get treats from their trainers. Others have figured out how to find their way through mazes.

Lemon sharks have even learned to hit targets with their noses, making bells go off, then swimming to another spot to be fed. Over time, they linked eating to the sound of the bells and swam directly to their feeding spot when they heard ringing.

Where in the World

OCEANS EVERYWHERE ARE HOME TO SHARKS—except, maybe, for the iciest Antarctic waters. Different kinds of sharks live in different parts of the world, but more kinds live in warm seas. Some prefer shallow water; others are mostly deep-sea fish. Some stay close to coasts; others swim in the open ocean. And bull sharks can live part of their lives in fresh water, such as the Mississippi River.

Angel sharks spend a lot of their time flat on the sea floor. They hide in sand that's the color of their skin. Divers who manage to spot them rarely see more than

A nurse shark can breathe without swimming. On the sea floor, it just opens and closes its mouth.

5

Traveling from deep, dark waters, a sixgill shark can rise swiftly toward the surface.

the sharks' eyes, which sit on the top of their heads.

During the day, swell sharks rest in underwater caves or narrow openings between rocks. They wedge themselves in place by swallowing a lot of water, making their bodies swell up. Occasionally, several swell sharks pile on top of one another.

Being wedged in a hiding place probably helps protect them from enemies, such as larger sharks.

Many sharks spend time traveling every day or every season. They're on the move to find more food or water temperatures that suit them. And female sharks often search for good nurseries—protected places for their young.

Some sharks move up and down between the depths and the shallows of the sea. Others swim from one coast to another.

COMING UP IN THE WORLD

In most parts of the world, scientists have to board submersibles to study sixgill sharks. These ancient fish normally live 1500 to 2500 metres (5000 to 8000 feet) down.

But each year, some of them visit a few spots along North America's west coast, often coming within 10 metres (33 feet) of the surface! Then scuba divers can swim with the sharks. Why these sixgills leave their deep-sea homes is a mystery no one has solved.

World in Motion

SWIMMING IS WHAT SHARKS DO BEST. Streamlined bodies and coverings of special scales let them slip easily through the water. And unlike most other fish, sharks have skeletons made—not of bone—but of cartilage. That's the material that shapes your ears and the tip of your nose. A cartilage skeleton bends easily and floats well, so sharks can move along with little effort.

Swimming power comes mostly from a shark's long tail and tail fins, which also help the fish make sudden turns. A thresher shark can use its tail—which is as long as

Besides being able to swim across oceans, the blue shark can dive deep.

9

A basking shark
moves slowly,
straining the
water for food.

its body—to herd and stun fish for food.
The one or two fins on a shark's back, plus
a pair near its back end, help keep the fish
upright in water. Its winglike side fins are
used for steering.

Not all sharks swim fast. Big basking
sharks and whale sharks just poke along as
they feed near the ocean's surface. But the

shortfin mako, one of the swiftest sharks at sea, can travel 35 kilometres (22 miles) an hour. The great white shark normally cruises slowly, saving its energy for short, high-speed attacks. When it's racing, it can leap right out of the water.

Some sharks are known for their long-distance swimming, not their speed. Blue sharks, for instance, often make huge trips. One swam all the way from New York to Brazil—a stretch of about 6000 kilometres (3725 miles)!

MONSTER EXPOSED!

Some monsters in sea yarns may really be basking sharks. Imagine as many as 50 of these giants—almost as long as whale sharks—sailing nose to tail. With only their top fins and a bit of their backs showing above water, they can appear to be one HUGE beast!

People also tell tales about dead basking sharks washing up on shore. Because their heads are small for their bodies, the sharks are often thought to be monsters—not big fish.

World of Senses

NOT MUCH GETS PAST A SHARK. Its senses are among the keenest of any animal. Although it has no outer ears, a shark hears well with its inner ears. Sound travels faster and farther through water than through air, so a shark can hear an injured seal or fish thrashing in the ocean more than a kilometre (a mile) away.

Because shark nostrils aren't used for breathing, they work full-time at sniffing. They can smell food that's a few city blocks away. Just the faint whiff of blood can attract a shark's attention.

Like other fish, a shark has a narrow

Sniff, sniff. The large nostrils of a sandbar shark draw smells from the water.

13

With clawlike parts, a copepod hooks onto the eye of a Greenland shark and feeds.

canal on each side of its head and body. Tiny hairs in these canals sense small movements and changes in pressure. They help the shark keep its balance and tell direction. They also work with its other senses, especially hearing, to find food.

No one is sure how far sharks can see, but they're able to use their eyes both day and night. In dim light, their sight seems to work better than a cat's.

Sensors in hundreds of pores on the front of a shark's head detect electricity, which all animals produce. As the shark closes in on food, it puts these sensors to work, even finding fish hidden in sand.

Some sharks also have feelers on their snouts for feeling and tasting food. And taste buds in their mouths and throats help sharks decide whether to swallow the food they catch or spit it out.

DEEP-SEA HITCHHIKERS

Tiny animals called copepods sometimes attach themselves to the eyes of Greenland sharks. As a copepod nibbles and scrapes an eye, it damages the sight of the shark.

The news isn't all bad for the shark, though. Because it lives mostly in the deep, dark waters of the Arctic and North Atlantic oceans, it doesn't depend much on its sight. The copepod might even attract fish that try to eat it. Then the Greenland shark can nab the fish.

Toothy World

SHARKS HAVE TEETH OUTSIDE AS WELL AS INSIDE. Their skin is covered with tiny scales, called denticles, that are built like teeth. These denticles are so sharp that they can scrape patches of skin off animals that rub against them. When they break or fall out, they're quickly replaced—throughout the shark's life.

Besides denticles, a shark grows a mouthful of teeth that vary according to the kind of shark. The teeth can be large or small, pointed or flat, smooth or rough, sharp or dull. Whale sharks have thousands of little, back-curving teeth set in more than

This mouth was made for chomping! The great white shark has strong jaws and sharp teeth.

17

New, curved teeth form in the jaw of a tiger shark. They can even bite through turtle shells.

300 rows. Great whites have long, pointed teeth with edges like bread knives. And cookie-cutter sharks—just the length of your arm—have teeth so sharp they've left marks on submarines!

Some sharks have combinations of different types of teeth. Bullhead sharks, for instance, have small, sharp front teeth for grabbing fish and big, dull back teeth for crushing shells on animals such as sea urchins.

Heavy-duty chomping can damage teeth, but that's no problem for a shark. Missing or broken teeth are replaced with spare ones that are always ready to move into place. During a single lifetime, a shark might lose and replace as many as 30 000 teeth! Like denticles, these teeth never grow, but each time they're replaced, the new ones are a size bigger.

SCALES TELL TALES

Teeth and denticles are often all that's left of sharks that lived a long time ago. During the 1990s, some of the oldest denticles ever found were discovered in sandstone in Colorado. Each was less than a millimetre ($\frac{1}{25}$ inch) long.

Scientists who examined the tiny tear-shaped denticles think they're probably about 450 million years old. They might possibly have belonged to ancient sharks so primitive they had suckerlike mouths—instead of jaws—with little teeth.

World Full of Food

OPENING W–I–D–E IS NO TROUBLE FOR A SHARK. Its jaws are loosely attached, making it easy for them to seize chunks of food. But the jaws don't move from side to side, so a shark can't chew its dinner. Instead, many sharks swallow food such as fish whole, and bite pieces off bigger animals.

What sharks eat depends a lot on their teeth. The tiny teeth of whale sharks are no good for piercing food, but these fish feed on small sea life floating in the water. The sharp teeth and strong jaws of cookie-cutter sharks can clamp onto the sides of animals

Whitetip reef sharks near Mexico gobble up fish and pull octopuses from their dens.

21

This spiny dogfish
shark might eat
a dinner of fish,
squid, and worms
—or become a
dinner for seals
or people.

as large as whales. These sharks earn their
name by twisting and turning to remove
circles of flesh.

Most sharks feed on several kinds of
animals, such as octopuses. Some kinds,
especially thresher sharks, nab whatever
they can—even turtles and birds. Sharks
push their stomachs out through their

mouths to throw up what they can't digest, such as turtle shells or hastily swallowed cans!

When they can, sharks may choose one food over another. Hammerheads prefer stingrays, and basking sharks like plankton. Despite tales of great white sharks hunting people, humans aren't their usual or favorite food. The sharks often spit them out.

Many sharks feed alone, but some hunt in packs. Thousands of spiny dogfish, for example, may attack a school of cod.

FILTERING FOOD

The sharks with the biggest mouths eat the smallest food. Whale, basking, and megamouth sharks all strain floating plants and animals—such as shrimp and copepods—from the sea. It's easy. The sharks simply open their mouths, and let the water flow in. It passes back out through "sieves" in the sharks' gills, where the food sticks until swallowed.

In only an hour, a basking shark can strain the plants and animals from 1800 tonnes (2000 tons) of water!

New World

SHALLOW WATER CAN MAKE GOOD NURSERIES—warm places rich with food for young sharks, called pups. When it's time to lay egg cases or give birth, many female sharks head for these nurseries.

Only a few sharks lay egg cases. Horn sharks anchor tough, screw-shaped cases in cracks between rocks. Swell sharks deposit purselike cases among seaweed. When swell shark pups are ready to hatch, they use special denticles to break free.

Many pups hatch from eggs that are kept inside their mothers. Then the little sharks feed mainly on their own egg yolks

A brown cat shark—as long as a man's arm—once hatched from an egg case the length of a man's nose.

25

Using nutrients from an attached yolk sac, a shark pup develops inside its egg case.

until they're ready to be born. Some kinds, such as sand tiger sharks, also feed on their brothers and sisters before birth!

Hammerhead, blue, and bull sharks carry their pups inside them—like mammals do. Until they're born, these pups are attached to their mother, getting all the nutrients they need from her.

Some sharks produce only one pup at a time. Others have many more. In 1995, though, scientists were shocked to find 300 pups growing inside a captured whale shark.

As soon as they're born, shark pups look after themselves. They're quite large and well developed. They can swim strongly enough to find food and flee from danger. But the pups grow up slowly. It usually takes many years before they're old enough to produce pups of their own.

SUPER SHARKS

Sharks are amazing! Here are just some of the reasons why:

- Shortfin mako sharks can leap about 6 metres (20 feet) out of the water.
- Shark skin is rough enough to be used as sandpaper and tough enough to be made into leather boots.
- Most sharks live fewer than 25 years, but some spiny dogfish sharks might survive for 100.

Index